RECEIVED

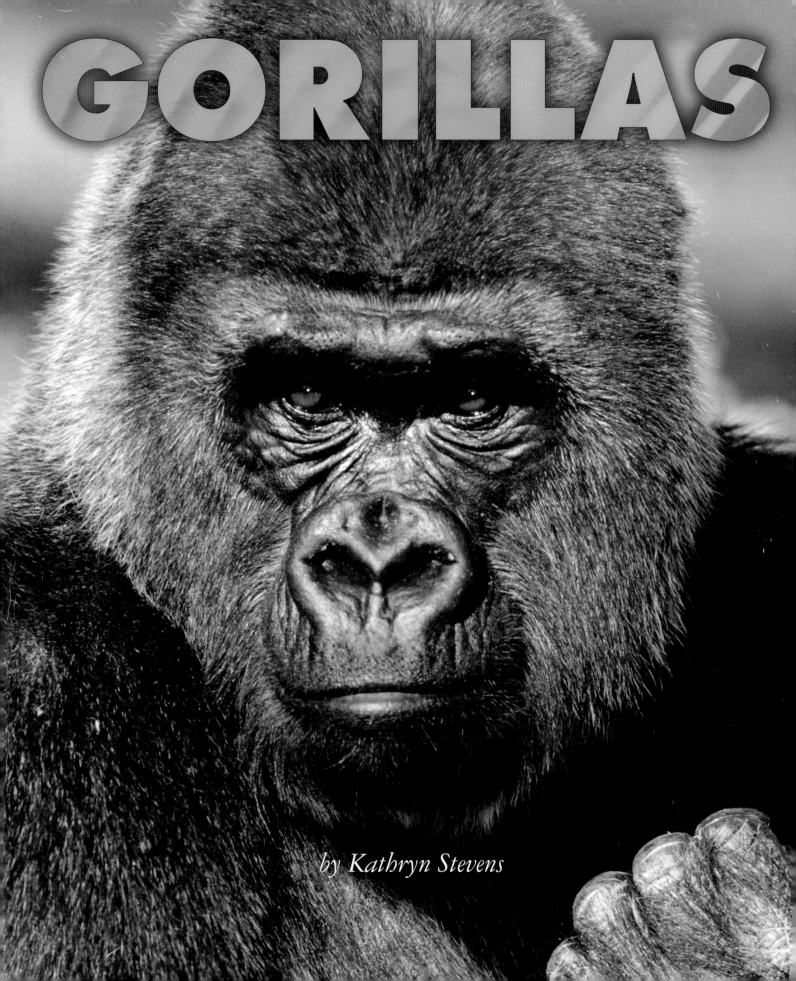

GORILLAS

by Kathryn Stevens

The Child's World

Our sincerest thanks to Dr. Patterson, Lorraine Slater, Dr. Cohn, and Koko for their assistance in making this book possible.

Published in the United States of America by The Child's World®
1980 Lookout Drive • Mankato, MN 56003-1705
800-599-READ • www.childsworld.com

PHOTO CREDITS
© Arco Images/Alamy: 9
© Cyril Ruoso/JH Editorial/Minden Pictures: 12
© Frans Lanting/Minden Pictures: cover, 1
© Fritz Polking/Dembinsky Photo Associates, Inc.: 14–15
© Gerry Ellis/Minden Pictures: 28
© Ingo Arndt/Minden Pictures: 17
© Joe McDonald/Animals Animals–Earth Scenes: 23
© Joe McDonald/Corbis: 4–5
© Karl Ammann/naturepl.com: 13
© Mike Lane/Alamy: 7
© Ron Cohn/Gorilla Foundation/koko.org: 24
© Steve Bloom Images/Alamy: 27
© Suzi Eszterhas/Minden Pictures: 21
© Suzi Eszterhas/naturepl.com: 18–19
© Tony Camacho/Photo Researchers, Inc.: 11

ACKNOWLEDGMENTS
The Child's World®: Mary Berendes, Publishing Director;
Katherine Stevenson, Editor; Pamela Mitsakos, Photo Researcher;
Judy Karren, Fact Checker

The Design Lab: Kathleen Petelinsek, Design; Kari Tobin, Page Production

LIBRARY OF CONGRESS CATALOGING-IN-PUBLICATION DATA
Stevens, Kathryn, 1954–
  Gorillas / by Kathryn Stevens.
      p. cm. — (New naturebooks)
  Includes index.
   ISBN 978-1-59296-846-6 (lib. bdg. : alk. paper)
  1. Gorilla—Juvenile literature. I. Title. II. Series.
  QL737.P96S745 2007
  599.884—dc22   200701582

Table of Contents

On the cover: This male western lowland gorilla is keeping a close eye on the photographer.

Meet the Gorilla!

Like people, gorillas have fingerprints—and no two gorillas' fingerprints are alike. Each gorilla has its own "noseprint," too. Scientist studying gorillas in the wild take close-up photos of the animals' faces. That helps them tell the animals apart.

Deep in an African forest, insects buzz in the afternoon heat. Birds are singing, but they're hard to see through all the leaves. You see some creatures in a clearing up ahead. From a distance, they look somewhat like shaggy humans! The bigger ones seem to be resting. Smaller ones are playing nearby. One big adult hears something. He stands up on two legs and looks around carefully. Seeing no danger, he settles down to rest again. When you get a better view, you can see that these creatures aren't human at all. They have long arms and leathery-looking faces, and their bodies are covered with hair. What are these forest animals? They're gorillas!

These mountain gorillas live in Rwanda's Volcanoes National Park.

What Do Gorillas Look Like?

All gorillas come from moist forest habitats. They live in the mountains and lowlands of western and central Africa.

Younger male gorillas that don't have patches of gray hair yet are called *blackbacks*.

Gorillas have big heads, big shoulders, and wide chests. Their arms are longer than their legs, and they have no tail. Their skin is dark, and their hair is black to reddish brown. They don't have hair on their faces, the palms of their hands, or the bottoms of their feet. They don't have much hair on their chests, either, especially if they're older males. As they get older, the gorillas' hair gets gray. Older males are called *silverbacks* because they get a big gray patch on their backs.

Gorillas are big! Males in the wild sometimes stand almost 6 feet (nearly 2 m) tall and weigh 400 pounds (181 kg). Males in zoos sometimes weigh even more. Female gorillas are a little shorter and weigh up to 200 pounds (91 kg).

You can see the huge arms on this western lowland gorilla.

What Are Gorillas?

Great apes are bigger and smarter than monkeys. They use their eyes more than their noses. They have fewer babies and take care of them for a longer time.

Gorillas' big toes act like thumbs. A gorilla can grasp things with its hands or its feet.

Gorillas are *primates*. That's a large animal group that includes people, apes, monkeys, lemurs, and some other animals. All primates are warm-bodied **mammals**. They have hair on their bodies, and the mothers produce milk for their babies. Gorillas are the biggest living members of a group of primates called *great apes*. Orangutans, chimpanzees, and bonobos are great apes, too.

Like other apes, gorillas sometimes stand on their hind legs. Usually gorillas do this to see better or to reach something. For walking, they use both their hands and their feet, with their fingers curled under their hands. This is called *knuckle walking*. Chimpanzees knuckle walk, too.

You can see how this female western lowland gorilla walks on her knuckles.

Are There Different Kinds of Gorillas?

Male western lowland gorillas have such large bony ridges that their heads look almost cone-shaped.

Gorillas living in the wild are hard to count. Once there were tens of thousands of western lowland gorillas. Their numbers have been dropping. No one is sure how many are left.

Scientist now believe that there are two main kinds, or **species**, of gorillas—western gorillas and eastern gorillas. Each species includes groups of animals that live in different areas. Some of these groups are different enough that scientists have given them separate names.

There are two types of western gorillas—Cross River gorillas and western lowland gorillas. Cross River gorillas are very rare. There are only about 200 left. They live in forested hills between Nigeria and Cameroon. Western lowland gorillas are much more common. They're the kind people see in zoos. In the wild, they live in several countries in western and central Africa. Western lowland gorillas use all types of forest habitats—rain forests, other dense forests, swampy areas, and forest edges and clearings. Their big, wide heads have heavy, bony ridges on the top and back and above the eyes. Their short, soft hair is perfect for the warm, moist forests where they live.

This Cross River gorilla lives at a wildlife center in Cameroon. How is this gorilla different from the ones on pages 5 and 7?

This eastern lowland gorilla is watching birds overhead in Kahuzi Biega, Congo.

There are two types of eastern gorillas, too. They're known as eastern lowland gorillas (also called Grauer's gorillas) and mountain gorillas. Eastern lowland gorillas live in **tropical** forests of the Congo area. Mountain gorillas are much better known, even though there are only about 700 of them left. Scientists have been studying two groups of mountain gorillas for many years. One group lives in mountain forests of the Virunga area. That's on the edge of the Democratic Republic of the Congo, Rwanda, and Uganda. The other group lives in the Bwindi area of Uganda. Higher areas of the mountain gorillas' homelands are cloudy and cool. The gorillas' blackish coats are long and thick to keep them warm.

This mountain gorilla is a silverback. He lives in Rwanda's Volcanoes National Park.

Mountain gorillas live in such wild areas that scientists didn't even know about them until 1902.

The Virunga area where mountain gorillas live is known for its volcanoes.

Some scientists think the Bwindi mountain gorillas are a separate type of eastern gorilla.

13

What Do Gorillas Eat?

Wild gorillas usually get all the water they need from the juicy plants they eat.

Western lowland gorillas live in areas with nearly a hundred different kinds of fruit.

Gorillas' big bellies hold lots of plant food while their bodies digest it.

Gorillas eat plant foods, and lots of them! Adult males can easily eat 40 pounds (18 kg) every day. Gorillas eat many kinds of plants, from vines and berries to bamboo and shrubs. They use their hands and mouths to pick their favorite parts. Those might be fruits, seeds, flowers, leaves, bark, roots, and even rotten wood. Big teeth and strong jaw muscles help the gorillas chew tough stems. Some gorillas also eat insects they come across, such as termites or ants.

Gorillas are **diurnal** animals that eat and move around during the day. In the morning they travel to a good source of food and eat their fill. Then they rest for a while. Later, they eat again until bedtime. The next morning, they move on to another place.

This mountain gorilla is munching on a plant in Rwanda.

14

How Do Gorillas Live?

Gorilla troops change over time, as some animals leave and new ones join.

When young females first leave their family troop, they find another one to join. Young males often live alone or with other males for a few years. A male can start his own troop if a female joins him.

Gorillas live in groups, or "troops," of only a few animals or up to 30. Each troop is led by a large, strong silverback male. The troop's other members are females and their young, and sometimes younger males. The silverback has a big job. He decides when and where the troop will travel. He decides when and where they will eat and rest. He keeps the troop safe from animals, hunters, and other gorilla troops. He helps keep peace within the group. He's usually the father of most of the troop's babies.

Gorillas live mostly peaceful lives. But sometimes silverbacks challenge each other. They charge and try to scare each other. Usually the smaller, weaker male backs down. Sometimes, though, the males actually fight. That can mean danger for females and babies nearby.

Here you can see a troop of mountain gorillas in Rwanda. The big silverback is making sure the photographer doesn't get too close.

Gorillas can climb, and youngsters often climb trees to play and find food. As the gorillas get bigger, they have to pick sturdy trees! Larger adults mostly stay on the ground. But even a big silverback might climb a tall tree to reach some tasty fruit. Because they're so heavy, adult males usually nest on or near the ground. Younger gorillas and females are more likely to nest in trees. When gorillas make nests, they sit in one spot and pull plants down around themselves. They bend the plants and weave them together to make a round nest. They never use the same nest twice.

A gorilla troop travels around within a home range. The animals move from one part to another to seek out different foods. They spend about a third of their day traveling and a third eating. The rest of the time they sleep or play.

This mountain gorilla mother and her baby are resting in their nest.

Some apes and other primates spend a lot of time grooming each other. They pick through each other's fur to remove dirt and bugs. Gorillas don't groom each other very much. Mothers often groom their young, though. And females sometimes groom the troop's silverback.

What Are Baby Gorillas Like?

A female gorilla can have a baby every four years or so. But only three of the babies might live to adulthood.

Silverback males can be good fathers. They sometimes raise young gorillas that lose their mothers. But if a new silverback takes over a troop, he might kill the old leader's babies.

A gorilla mother usually has one only baby at a time. Weighing only 4 to 5 pounds (about 2 kg), gorilla newborns are even smaller than most human babies! At first, the mother carefully holds and carries her baby. But in a couple of months, the baby is strong enough to hold onto its mother's hair. Then it learns to ride on her back. The baby can walk at five or six months. But for moving through the forest, riding on the mother's back is safer.

The young gorilla learns by watching older gorillas and by playing with other youngsters. It stops drinking its mother's milk when it is about three years old. But it stays close to its mother until it is at least four. Gorillas become adults when they are seven or eight. Then they are ready to leave their family group.

This baby mountain gorilla is about ten months old.

How Do Gorillas Communicate?

In the dense forest, it can be hard for gorillas to see each other. Making sounds helps them stay in touch.

Sounds and body movements help gorillas settle problems without fighting.

When a gorilla is feeling stressed, it yawns. When it is angry, it bares its teeth or clenches them tight.

Gorillas are smart. They have lots of ways of communicating with each other. Scientists have heard them make over 20 different sounds. Usually gorillas are fairly quiet, making soft grunting or belching noises. But sometimes they scream, bark, or roar. Silverbacks tend to be the noisiest.

Gorillas communicate in other ways, too. They make faces by sticking out their tongues, yawning, or sucking in their lips. These different faces have meanings. Gorillas also communicate with body movements. Males sometimes charge at people or other gorillas they want to scare. They hoot, then pretend to eat. They stand on their hind legs and throw plants. They slap their chests and kick. They run sideways and tear at nearby plants. To finish, they hit their hands on the ground.

This western lowland gorilla is beating his chest. Chest beating is a way for gorillas to show anger or excitement.

Some gorillas have learned to communicate with people, too! Over thirty years ago, a year-old gorilla named Koko started learning human sign language. She also learned to understand spoken English words. People would speak aloud, and she would answer in signs. Today Koko knows over 1,000 signs and 2,000 spoken words. Michael, a male gorilla raised with Koko, learned over 600 signs before he died. Scientists have different views on how much gorillas really understand about language. But they are interested to learn more about how gorillas and many other animals communicate. And one thing is certain—Koko and Michael have changed people's ideas about what gorillas can do!

Here Koko is making the sign for "have." She makes this sign when she wants something.

Gorillas' hands aren't shaped like people's hands. Koko uses her own Gorilla Sign Language. It's slightly different from American Sign Language.

Koko has cared for her own pet cats.

Both Koko and Michael learned to enjoy painting pictures.

Are Gorillas in Danger?

People in many parts of Africa eat "bushmeat." That's the meat of any kind of wild animal. People are now hunting more wildlife to sell the bushmeat. Scientists now see this as one of the biggest dangers to Africa's wildlife, including gorillas.

Gorillas are some of the most **endangered** animals on Earth. The number of people in Africa keeps growing. Logging, mining, and farming have destroyed huge areas of forest habitat. Hunters have killed countless gorillas for meat or to sell their body parts. Gorillas die from traps meant for other animals. Babies are caught illegally to sell as pets. Gorillas also catch some of the same diseases people do. One disease called *ebola* has been killing people, chimpanzees, and gorillas. It has killed at least several thousand gorillas in recent years. People and governments have been fighting in these regions, too. It's hard for anyone to protect gorillas, even when they live in parks.

This silverback is the leader of a small troop of mountain gorillas. They live in Uganda's Mgahinga National Park.

No one is certain whether some gorilla populations can still be saved. Protecting gorillas means saving the forests where they live. But people who live in those areas need food and jobs, too. Sometimes there are ways to help both the people and the animals. For example, visitors from other countries love to see wildlife. Their visits bring money and jobs for local people. Then the local people have more reasons to help protect the wildlife.

There are a few success stories. In 10 years, the number of mountain gorillas in the Virunga area grew from 324 to 380. That's because people were keeping a close watch on these animals, trying to keep them safe. Lots of people care about gorillas and what happens to them. They hope to keep these gentle giants safe in their forest homes!

Scientists are studying gorillas both in the wild and in zoos. There is still a lot to learn about these intelligent animals.

Gorillas can live to be about 35 years old in the wild. They often live longer in zoos. The oldest known zoo gorilla died at age 54.

This baby mountain gorilla was very curious about the photographer's camera. He and his troop live in Rwanda's Virunga Mountains.

Glossary

digest (DY-jest) To digest food is to break it down into smaller, simpler pieces that the body can use. Gorillas bodies' digest all kinds of plant foods.

diurnal (dy-UR-null) An animal that is diurnal is active mostly during the day and rests at night. Gorillas are diurnal.

endangered (in-DAYN-jurd) An endangered animal is one that is close to dying out completely. Gorillas are endangered.

habitats (HA-bih-tats) Animals' habitats are the types of surroundings in which the animals live. Many areas of gorilla habitat have been destroyed.

mammals (MAM-ullz) Mammals are warm-blooded animals that have hair on their bodies and feed their babies milk from the mother's body. Gorillas are mammals.

species (SPEE-sheez) An animal species is a group of animals that share the same features and have babies only with animals in the same group. There are two species of gorillas.

tropical (TRAH-pih-kull) Tropical areas are those that have warm, moist weather all year long. Gorillas live in Africa's tropical forests.

To Find Out More

Watch It!

The Gorilla Foundation. *Koko's Kitten*. VHS. Los Angeles: Churchill Films, 1989.

Mountain Gorilla. DVD. Burbank, CA: Warner Home Video, 2002.

National Geographic Society. *Gorilla*. VHS. Stamford, CT: Vestron Video, 1986.

PBS Nature: A Conversation with Koko. New York: Thirteen/WNET, 1999.

Read It!

Brend, Stephen. *Gorilla: Habitats, Life Cycles, Food Chains, Threats*. Natural World. Austin, TX: Raintree Steck-Vaughn, 2003.

Johnston, Marianne. *Gorillas and Their Babies*. New York: PowerKids Press, 1999.

Patterson, Francine, and Ronald H. Cohn (photographer). *Koko's Kitten*. New York, Scholastic, 1985.

Simon, Seymour. *Gorillas*. New York: HarperCollins, 2000.

Turner, Pamela S. *Gorilla Doctors: Saving Endangered Great Apes*. Boston, MA: Houghton Mifflin, 2005.

On the Web

Visit our Web page for lots of links about gorillas:
http://www.childsworld.com/links

Note to Parents, Teachers, and Librarians: We routinely check our Web links to make sure they're safe, active sites—so encourage your readers to check them out!

31

Index

About the Author

Kathryn Stevens is an archaeologist as well as an editor and author of numerous children's books on nature and science, geography, and other topics. She lives in western Wisconsin, where she spends her spare time enjoying the outdoors, restoring a Victorian house, and making pet-therapy visits with her dog.